CRYSTAL CLEAR

CRYSTAL CLEAR

The Story of Diamonds

Victor Argenzio

DAVID McKAY COMPANY, INC.
NEW YORK

Library of Congress Cataloging in Publication Data

Argenzio, Victor.
  Crystal clear.

  SUMMARY: Describes the formation, properties, and
uses of diamonds, where they are found, how they are
cut, and stories of the great diamonds of the world.
  1. Diamonds—Juvenile literature. [1. Diamonds]
I. Title.
TS753.A68   553'.82   76-16347
ISBN 0-679-20317-6

                10 9 8 7 6 5 4 3 2 1
        MANUFACTURED IN THE UNITED STATES OF AMERICA

To John Burls

Preface

Before starting this book, I thought it might be a good idea to investigate what students might like to know about diamonds. The question "What do you want to know about diamonds?" was asked in a number of schools throughout the country. It brought many and varied replies. A high degree of intelligence was expected, and was forthcoming.

Much of what is contained in this book is a direct result of the answers received.

I sincerely thank the school officials, the teachers, and the hundreds of pupils who cooperated so willingly in response to my survey.

Contents

CRYSTAL
CLEAR

The Kohinoor diamond—replicas before and after re-fashioning. (N.W. Ayer & Son, Inc.)

The History of Diamonds

Nadir Shah, the barbarous king of the Persians, invaded the lovely city of Delhi in 1739. The head of one of the most brutal armies of all time, he plundered the great palaces and temples of the Moguls of India.

More than anything else, Nadir Shah wanted to get his hands on the Kohinoor diamond, known to be in Delhi. He had heard that "He who owns the Kohinoor rules the world."

But the diamond was nowhere to be found. He ordered his men to kill and torture until the jewel was located. For almost two months his search failed to bring the great stone out of hiding. In his rage Nadir burned palaces, public buildings, and much of the city. His men cleaned out everything they saw, like an army of locusts in a field of crops.

Finally, Nadir resorted to trickery, learned where the Kohinoor was hidden, and soon had it for his own. This diamond, now among the Crown Jewels of England, was the most famous of its time, as it still is today.

Many of the world's famous diamonds have histories steeped in violence and bloodshed, while others have pasts associated with treachery, superstition, and famous robberies. Perhaps this all adds to the glamour of diamonds.

Ever since they were first discovered in India, around 800 B.C., diamonds have had an air of mystery and romance about them. From the very start, they took their place as highly prized gems, and they were eagerly collected by the ruling potentates of their time. This was long before their exquisite beauty was brought out by cutting and polishing.

Diamonds have been the chief attraction of royal crowns, an emblem of power for the heads of State. They have ransomed kings and kingdoms. In later years, they have saved untold thousands from their enemies by being bargained for their lives. They have been the cause of tragedy and grief and death for some, a source of pride and happiness for others. Most important, they have performed the most demanding jobs of industry.

What is the nature of a jewel that is owned and treasured by more persons than all the other precious gems combined?

The Nature of Diamonds

Diamonds are rare, being found in only a few parts of the world. They are extremely hard, and after they are cut and polished, their brilliance and beauty are unequaled. Their value as gems, for these reasons, has continued to increase throughout the years.

Structure

Diamonds are practically pure carbon. Carbon is one of the earth's natural elements and comes in two solid forms, graphite and diamonds. The differences in these two forms result from the differences in their structure. Graphite does not require high pressure for its formation, and the atoms lie loosely in sheets that slide easily over each other. Graphite provides us with such things as lubricants and pencil leads. But the diamond, formed under very high heat and pressure, is made up of carbon atoms that are packed in the very tightest possible way and in the most orderly manner. So tightly are the atoms packed and with so little space between them that a diamond of a given size will weigh more than twice that of graphite of the same size.

Hardness

The diamond, crystallized under tremendous heat and pressure, comes forth as the hardest natural material known to man. One of the most awesome and fascinating aspects of the diamond is its very hardness. Not too long ago, this was dramatized when a fairly large rough diamond was pushed with ease through a sheet of steel. *That is hard!*

The word *diamond* comes from the Greek word *adamas,* meaning invincible. The first-century philosopher Pliny the Elder stated that a good way to check the hardness of a diamond was to hit it with a hammer. This is not true, however. Each diamond has a structure that might be compared to that of a piece of wood. If a diamond is struck along the lines of its "grain," it can be split the same way as a piece of wood properly struck. We can be sure that the diamond that pierced the sheet of steel was set very carefully, or the steel might well have won that test of strength.

Cleavage

When a diamond is split before the sawing process, which it sometimes is, the operation is called cleaving. Some very large diamonds, like the Cullinan, were first cleaved and then sawed.

If a diamond is hit sharply against a hard object, the diamond may chip, break, or become badly damaged on account of being struck along its line of cleavage. While this does not happen often, it can happen; so the diamond, like any valuable object, must be treated with care.

A classic example of the destruction of a diamond is the story of the great Pigot diamond. In 1822, the owner, Ali Pasha, was mortally wounded in a battle. As he lay dying in his throne room, he ordered the destruction of two of his most precious possessions—his wife, Vasiliki, and his diamond—to keep them from his enemies. The great diamond was pulverized before his eyes, but luckily he died before his wife could be killed, and she escaped. According to some historians, this is the only known instance of a famous diamond being purposely destroyed.

Recently there have been reports of diamonds being destroyed in garbage disposals. It's hard to believe, but experts seem to believe that the grinding action of the disposal acts just like the cleaving process, and the diamonds are cleaved over and over until only tiny chips are left.

Very high heat can damage a diamond. A diamond can withstand ordinary fire without too much damage; but if the temperature gets too hot, it may become clouded and dull, a condition that can be remedied by polishing the gem. Really high temperatures, such as might result from airplane disasters, have badly damaged diamonds.

So the diamond is not invincible. Even though it is the hardest mineral known, it is brittle and will cleave readily when struck and will burn in air at 1000 degrees Centigrade (1832 degrees Fahrenheit).

Diamonds can also wear out. Once a 19-carat industrial diamond was used in an American automobile factory. In the sixteen years that the stone was used, it wore down to a quarter of a carat.

Weight

Despite their high unit value, diamonds are measured by weight, like meat or potatoes, although weight is only one factor that determines their value. The others are cutting, color, and purity. The basic unit of weight is a carat. The word *carat* comes from *carob,* a small Oriental bean so uniform in size that it was used to weigh gems in ancient times. *Carat* is different from *karat,* which measures the fineness of gold. A carat is 1/142 of an ounce, or 200

Carob seeds, which are remarkably uniform in weight—the basis of the carat. (Jewelers Circular-Keystone.)

milligrams. Each carat is divided into one hundred parts, like our dollar, so we read a weight of 3.42 ct. or 143.76 ct. and so on. To get an idea of size, a well-proportioned round-cut diamond of one carat is almost exactly one quarter of an inch in diameter. That is not very large, but its value can vary anywhere from $100 or less to well over $7,500, according to its quality.

It takes 4,544,000 carats to make a ton, and about ten tons are recovered each year. Of these, only about 25 percent are of gem quality; the rest are used in industry. The demand for both gem and industrial qualities far outstrips the supply, and this accounts for the high cost of diamonds.

The largest diamond ever found, the Cullinan, weighed in its original state an unbelievable 3,106 carats. This comes to one and one third pounds, a more understandable idea of weight. It was about the size of the fist of a good-sized man. When it was cut, the great diamond yielded not only the world's largest cut diamond but also the second largest, as well as many others. The two largest are on display with other Crown Jewels in the Tower of London, in England. Large diamonds are particularly rare. Most diamonds are small, and the very smallest are like grains of sand.

Color

Pure diamonds have no color of their own. The very finest colorless diamonds may be compared to a drop of distilled water, totally without color except for the rainbow hues that it flashes as it separates white light into the colors of the spectrum.

The Cullinan rough. (Asscher Diamond Cutting Works, Amsterdam.)

Diameters and Corresponding Weights of
Round, Ideally Proportioned, Brilliant-Cut Diamonds

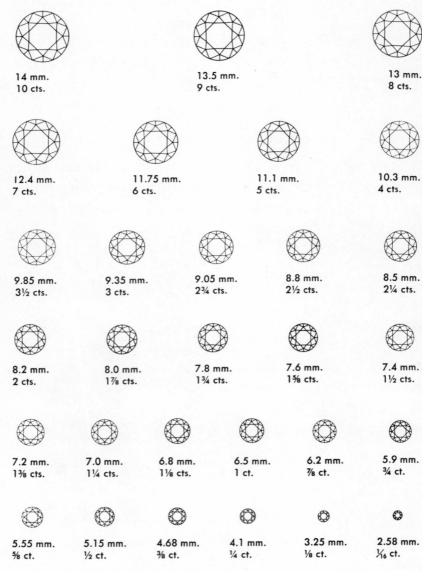

14 mm.
10 cts.

13.5 mm.
9 cts.

13 mm.
8 cts.

12.4 mm.
7 cts.

11.75 mm.
6 cts.

11.1 mm.
5 cts.

10.3 mm.
4 cts.

9.85 mm.
3½ cts.

9.35 mm.
3 cts.

9.05 mm.
2¾ cts.

8.8 mm.
2½ cts.

8.5 mm.
2¼ cts.

8.2 mm.
2 cts.

8.0 mm.
1⅞ cts.

7.8 mm.
1¾ cts.

7.6 mm.
1⅝ cts.

7.4 mm.
1½ cts.

7.2 mm.
1⅜ cts.

7.0 mm.
1¼ cts.

6.8 mm.
1⅛ cts.

6.5 mm.
1 ct.

6.2 mm.
⅞ ct.

5.9 mm.
¾ ct.

5.55 mm.
⅝ ct.

5.15 mm.
½ ct.

4.68 mm.
⅜ ct.

4.1 mm.
¼ ct.

3.25 mm.
⅛ ct.

2.58 mm.
¹⁄₁₆ ct.

Sizes of round diamonds from 10 carats to 1/16 carat. (Gemological Institute of America.)

Very, very few diamonds are colorless. By far, most have some color, such as yellow or brown. Color in diamonds is caused by the presence of impurities, usually very tiny quantities of nitrogen trapped inside. The more yellow or brown the stone, the less the value. Diamonds are sometimes found in green, pink, rose, or other colors. These are known as "fancies" and can command the highest prices.

When diamonds are found in their original state, called rough, they are not always pretty. Often, they have a "skin" that gives them a dirty, unattractive appearance. When this layer is polished off, however, a transparent gem will be found.

Pricing

In all the world, about twelve or thirteen million carats of gem diamonds are recovered annually. By the time they are cut, this amount will be halved owing to the loss in the cutting and fashioning processes. Thus, diamonds used for jewelry are very valuable.

Large diamonds are the rarest. This is reflected in their pricing: the scarcer the objects, the costlier they are. For instance, if we take a 1-carat round diamond of fine quality, it might sell for $5,000, but a 2-carat stone of like quality would be priced at $15,000 or over.

How Diamonds Were Formed

Diamonds were formed deep within the earth millions of years ago, crystallized from carbon into the world's hardest mineral. Recent experiments indicate that temperatures in the range of 5000 degrees Fahrenheit must have been required, with pressures of more than a million pounds per square inch. This heat and pressure could have been possible only in the seething, boiling mass of molten rock in the mantle of the earth, the fluid mass under the earth's crust. It is thought likely that the action took place at depths of from eighty to one hundred twenty-five miles below the surface.

It is not known precisely how the diamonds were formed. Possibly the molten mass started pushing upward through the weakest areas of the rock structure. As time elapsed, the fluid cooled sufficiently to permit diamond crystals to grow, much like the way in which salt and sugar crystals form in a cooling water solution.

No one knows how long it took nature to form diamonds. Some claim that it took thousands or even millions of years. But now that the General Electric Company has succeeded in growing synthetic gem diamonds in a very short interval of time, we may be permitted to question some of the old theories. We do know from the dating methods used today that the diamonds now being mined were formed millions of years ago. But the question arises, *What is there to prevent the same conditions from taking place even now?*

Another question that has been answered in several ways

Diamonds were formed under tremendous heat and pressure when the world was young. (De Beers Consolidated Mines, Ltd.)

but remains most interesting is, *How did that molten mass get through the barrier of solid, granitelike rocks ranging in thickness from twenty-five to thirty-five miles in continents where diamonds have been found, such as Africa?*

One recently projected theory is that the upward drive was caused by natural rocket power, sudden lift-offs so great that they make our Apollos seem like baby firecrackers by comparison.

The molten material blasted through cracks and fissures and weak spots in the rock structure until it exploded through the top of the surface with a mighty roar. Some of these eruptions formed volcanoes, and the deposits left the diamonds close to the top, where they congealed into a hard mass of igneous rock. Kimberlite, the only known source rock of diamonds, is an igneous rock. The masses that solidified in the necks of the volcanoes are called pipes and extend deep down through the earth's crust.

Not all the volcanic pipes contained diamonds, and we wonder how many diamonds made their way to the surface, and how many never did. Is it possible that parts of the earth's interior are studded with diamonds that will never get any further than where they are now trapped below? Perhaps we shall never know.

Through the centuries, the forces of erosion have been at work. The action of torrential rains, temperature changes, the changing course of rivers, the gouging of glaciers, and other forces have worn the mountains down to the level of the plains. Gradually the diamonds in their beds of kimberlite have been uncovered—at least some of them. Ancient rivers and glacial ice have transported them far from their point of origin. The diamonds, because of their hardness, survived this merciless battering and were scattered over many areas of the world.

Even today more diamonds are recovered far from the pipes of their origin than are mined within them. In the mines themselves, the miners find fewer diamonds as they go deeper.

Where Diamonds Are Found

Nature has been coy in the way she has allowed her valuable diamond deposits to be found. First, there was India. Tremendous quantities were discovered there, and most of the diamonds that were to become very famous came from that country—the Kohinoor, the Hope, the Great Mogul, the Orloff, the Sancy, and the Regent, to name but a few.

The great mines of India finally gave out after 2,500 years of mining. But just about that time, diamonds were discovered in Brazil when, by accident, miners learned that the pebbles they were using for gambling tallies were real diamonds. Great excitement followed. This was in 1726. For almost 150 years, Brazil was the diamond center of the world. Slowly but surely, diamond mining here also came to almost a complete halt, and the world had lost another major source.

But not for long. In 1866, children of a farmer near Hopetown, South Africa, were playing with a beautiful pebble. Luckily, they didn't throw it away. It proved to be a diamond. Three years later another one was found in the same area—a big and valuable one. That brought a tremendous rush into the area. South Africa had hit the jackpot. Diamonds in quantities never heard of before were uncovered, changing the diamond picture of the world. For the first time ever, people other than the very wealthy were able to buy these precious stones. Even today, Africa is known as the diamond continent, with South Africa and other African nations producing three quarters of the world's supply.

Now the Soviet Union has entered the picture. The Russians have found diamond-bearing pipes in Siberia—as many as have been found in Africa. The Soviets do not give out figures of their production too willingly, but it has been estimated that they mined almost one quarter of the world total in 1975, and they claim that in a short time they will lead the world in diamond output.

A view of a Siberian diamond mine showing workers digging in the frozen ground. (His Excellency Mr. Arnold Smith.)

There used to be considerable speculation about the possibility of finding diamonds on the moon, but nothing brought back to earth by our astronauts gives the slightest evidence of it.

Scientists fairly well agree that all the continents were joined together at one time, so it is possible that new diamond discoveries may be made in unexpected places. Alaska and Canada must be considered possible sources. Canadian provinces have been studying areas around the Hudson Bay region for years.

The market for diamonds keeps getting bigger, and we must wait and see how nature reveals new hiding places to help keep up with the demand for these gems.

Diamonds in the United States

The United States, so rich in many resources, was overlooked when it came to diamonds. However, a few have been found, and like all other nations, we hope someday to strike it rich. Scattered diamonds have been picked up in several states, from New York to California. Quite a few have turned up in the Great Lakes area, mostly small but including one over 15 carats and another over 21 carats. No one knows where these diamonds originated; possibly they were pushed down by a tremendous upheaval during the Ice Age thousands of years ago. The area in the Appalachian Mountains has produced many, including a few of fairly good size. Again, their origin is a mystery; there may be hidden pipes somewhere that might come to light someday.

Arkansas has the only diamond-bearing pipe in North America that has produced diamonds in quantities. Called the "Crater of Diamonds," it is located in Murfreesboro. The largest diamond ever found in the United States came from there, the "Uncle Sam," weighing over 40 carats—a very big one for this country.

Much money was spent to produce diamonds commercially at the Murfreesboro mine, but it never did pay off. Just the same, over 60,000 diamonds have been found since its discovery in 1906. The state of Arkansas took over the mine

The Crater of Diamonds State Park in Murfreesboro, Arkansas, where finders are keepers. (Little Rock State Parks Recreation and Travel Commission.)

in 1972 as a tourist attraction, and for a small fee anyone can dig all day and keep what he or she finds. Some good-sized stones have been unearthed recently, including a whopper of over 16 carats. It was found in August 1975 by a Texan, and the diamond is reported to be of fine quality, and therefore a very valuable stone.

An interesting and exciting development occurred in 1975 when the U. S. Geological Survey announced that it had uncovered tiny diamond crystals in the south central part of Wyoming. These were found in real kimberlite pipes that extend to northern Colorado. The crystals measure but one millimeter across (1/25 inch). Much time and research will be spent to determine if diamonds might be found in quantities sufficient to justify large-scale probing and operations. Whatever the outcome, it is the most important diamond news in the United States for many years.

The unexpected announcement by the U. S. Geological Survey about the discovery of tiny diamonds in Wyoming pipes that extend to northern Colorado just has to remind us that the greatest diamond hoax of all time took place at almost the same location a hundred years ago.

It was at the time that South Africa was making headlines with its huge diamond finds—a topic of interest the world over—that two miners appeared in a San Francisco bank with a bag of rough diamonds and said to one and all that

Mrs. Thomas W. Evener of Golden, Colorado, holding a diamond she found. (The Nashville *News, Nashville, Arkansas.)*

they had found a diamond mine and wanted to leave a few samples on display. But they refused to tell where the mine was located. The diamonds caused a great sensation, as the miners knew they would. The two were offered a great sum if they would lead a few selected persons to the site. Under excited prodding they agreed, but on condition that the prospectors be blindfolded until they got to the fields. When they arrived and the blindfolds were removed, sure enough there were diamonds all over the place! Again blindfolded, the prospectors returned to California; and when the news got out, dozens of companies were formed, with millions of dollars in capital appropriated to exploit the affair. The bankers called in the leading engineer of the day, and he, too, was blindfolded and taken to the secret hideaway. Like the others, he returned with the news that this was indeed a fabulous occurrence. The diamonds were checked by the famous New York jewelers Tiffany & Company. They were real all right, and New York capital, along with famous names, all clambered onto the bandwagon. Even European money followed.

The two miners were not too happy with the way things were getting out of their hands. Consequently, when they were offered hundreds of thousands of dollars for their share and were advised to leave, they did.

Finally, geologist Clarence King, who later became the first head of the Geological Survey, decided to make an investigation of his own, as the "mine" was in his territory. He soon realized that the diamonds, of cheap quality, had been planted by humans and not nature, and that there *was* no diamond mine. He hurried back to San Francisco to warn everyone. Great losses by investors were avoided by his disclosures.

The two miners must have laughed to think how they had fooled all those smart bankers and millionaires.

This story has been told and retold, and even today—a hundred years later—it is discussed, written about, and re-created on television.

Recovery of Diamonds

The recovery of diamonds can be very simple or very complex. When they were first found in 800 B.C., diamonds were literally picked up from the ground. They still are. In India it was reported that in the seventeenth century, as many as 50,000 men, women, and children worked under the hot sun, carrying the gravel to creeks for washing so that the diamonds could be picked out by hand. Ever present were guards armed with whips who spurred on the workers and made sure that all diamonds found were turned in. The gems were so plentiful that very crude methods were all that was needed.

When diamonds were discovered in South Africa in 1866, the methods of recovery had changed but little. The miners thought at first that the diamonds all lay in shallow ground. When they learned that many were deep in the earth, the miners changed their methods. They dug deeper and deeper; roads caved in, mine walls collapsed, and fights broke out over claim rights. Soon they struck water, and shafts were flooded. As the digging got deeper, the danger of being injured by falling walls, or even of being buried alive, intensified. But the lure of riches overcame all thoughts of peril.

When the first pipe mine was discovered in South Africa in 1870, more advanced ways of extracting the diamonds became necessary. A vertical shaft was sunk into the ground parallel to each of the pipes, sometimes as much as 1,000 feet away. At intervals of forty feet or so, horizontal tunnels

The "Big Hole" at Kimberley, showing the shape of the diamond-bearing volcanic "pipe" that was one of the first diamond mines in South Africa. (N.W. Ayer & Son, Inc.)

were drilled into the kimberlite, which was then blasted loose and trundled out to mine cars. Elevators took the ore to the surface to treatment plants. There the blue ground (kimberlite) was screened for size, the large pieces being carried by belts to the crushers to be broken into smaller

Deep down in the Premier mine, a crew prepares to blast out a section of diamond-bearing "blue ground." (N.W. Ayer & Son, Inc.)

Underground in a Kimberley mine, a conveyor belt carries broken blue ground. Diamonds are deeply embedded in these pieces. (N.W. Ayer & Son, Inc.)

This crusher recovers diamonds from the blue ground. (N.W. Ayer & Son, Inc.)

pieces. Then the crushed material was mixed with water in huge washers and stirred by metal rakes.

The ore was then put into huge tanks of a special liquid, with a specific gravity slightly less than that of a diamond, which is 3.52. This means that a diamond is just about three and one half times as heavy as the same volume of water. This special liquid allows the lighter waste materials to be floated off, while the heavier materials, including any diamonds, sink to the bottom to be recovered.

An unusual characteristic of a diamond is its attraction to grease. More advanced ways of separating diamonds from other matter are used in diamond mines these days, but formerly diamonds and other matter were put on a revolving belt covered with a layer of grease. Water washed over everything, and all waste and foreign matter disappeared, but the diamonds stuck to the grease, making their recovery simple.

After the diamonds are recovered, they are cleaned and sorted. The poorer qualities are to be used in industry; the gem-quality diamonds go to the cutting works.

Mines are worked to great depths; the Kimberley mine got down to 3,600 feet, over two thirds of a mile.

Different procedures are used at the great Consolidated Diamond Mines of South-West Africa, where more fine quality diamonds are found than anywhere else on earth. Here the diamonds are buried under vast sand dunes, and millions of tons of sand must be removed to get to the diamonds. Although a never-ending battle between man and the sea, it is well worthwhile because it is the most profitable operation of its kind.

Diamonds are also recovered from the sea itself. Barges complete with machinery to suck the diamonds from the sea are also equipped to process the diamonds right on board.

Another story of diamond recovery that borders on the incredible is the way diamonds are mined in Siberia. The eight-month-long winters can get to −70 degrees Fahrenheit. The permafrost, a permanently frozen layer at variable depths below the earth's surface in frigid regions, can get to be hundreds of feet in depth. It must be warmed before it can be dug. The success of the Soviets in keeping machinery going in these extremely cold zones is an engineering feat in itself.

Cutting Diamonds

Rough crystals come in many shapes, and each shape defines the form in which the diamond will be cut—round (brilliant cut), oval, marquise (pronounced mar-KEYS), emerald cut, or other. The diamond cutter's task is to take the unattractive gem and turn it into a beautiful sparkling jewel. When a diamond is properly cut, it is the most beautiful of all gemstones. The diamond was given numerous advantages by nature in its construction, but it took the cutters many years to learn how to take advantage of them by proper cutting.

Much of the diamond's beauty comes from its ability to bend the light rays entering it. This is called refraction, and each gem has its own index of refraction, which is determined by the internal structure of the mineral itself. The index of refraction is based on the change in the speed of light as it enters the stone. Diamonds have the highest index of refraction of the valuable gemstones, 2.42. The refractive index of an emerald is 1.585, and the corundum jewels—ruby and sapphire—only slightly higher, 1.760.

The speed of light is approximately 186,000 miles per second. In the case of the diamond, that speed is reduced, due to refraction, to 76,860 miles per second. This gives us a reading of $186,000 \div 76,860 = 2.42$.

The cutter's knowledge and skill make the diamond a light trap by taking advantage of its power to absorb and bend the entering light rays and send back to the eye all possible brilliance and beauty. A diamond also has the ability to

Diamonds in the rough are transformed into brilliant gems through the process of cutting. Rough diamonds may take a variety of shapes, as shown here. (N.W. Ayer & Son, Inc.)

separate white light into the colors of the spectrum in a process known as dispersion. It is what gives the diamond so much of its beauty.

In India, where diamonds were first found, the only way of improving their appearance was to rub one against another to obtain a sort of polish. Long ago it was learned that only a diamond can cut a diamond. So the diamond was put on a revolving wheel smeared with diamond dust and oil, and crude facets were ground into shape in this way. Not until the eighteenth century was it learned that a diamond could be sawed. Far better than grinding, this method wasted much less material.

Great strides were made in the fifteenth century, when

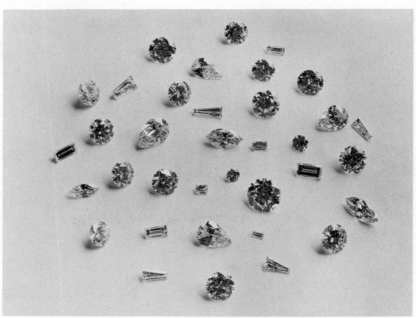

A selection of finished diamonds at Goldmuntz Polishing Works, Antwerp. (Goldmuntz Polishing Works.)

Belgian artisan Louis de Berquem made tremendous improvements in the art of cutting a diamond. He went to Paris to study mathematics, so important in the proper placing and angling of the facets (flat planes on the stone). A statue of this master cutter stands in a public square in Antwerp.

Another great name in diamond cutting history is Vincenti Peruzzi, a Venetian cutter of the seventeenth century. It was he who came up with a "brilliant" of fifty-eight facets, the forerunner of the cut used the world over today, with only slight changes and improvements.

Diamonds are first divided, usually by sawing. Then they are "girdled," which means rounded and shaped at their

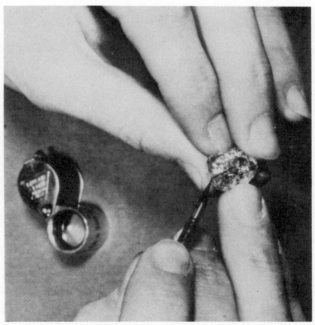

An expert examines a diamond through a powerful magnifying glass—the loupe shown above—to see how the stone can be cut for maximum weight. After studying the stone's imperfections, he marks the diamond where it must be divided. (N.W. Ayer & Son, Inc.)

The characteristic diamond shape is an octahedron, roughly like two four-sided pyramids stuck together, base to base.

The rough stone is sawed into two parts.

Next it is "rounded" by grinding the corners away.

Then, when 58 facets have been polished on the rounded stone, the result is the standard brilliant cut.

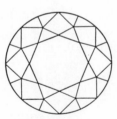

Top—33 facets

Side view

Bottom—25 facets

greatest width. The final step is cutting the facets, which is responsible for bringing out the optical properties of the stones. The facets are carefully placed and angled, and the polishing and final minor corrections complete the job.

While more and more cutting is done mechanically, the end result must come from the unerring eye and skill of the cutters who guide the many steps.

Countless stones have been spoiled or ruined by poor cutting. The most notable was the Great Mogul. An inept Venetian cutter reduced the great stone from 787.5 carats to 280 carats and then turned out a terrible job.

The famous Kohinoor was recut at the request of Queen Victoria, who thought it didn't have enough brilliancy. This famous diamond was reduced from 186 carats to 108.93 carats. Not only did the operation fail to bring out the expected brilliancy but the stone no longer resembled the diamond that had made history.

Fluorescent lights do little to bring out a diamond's brilliancy. Incandescent lights are much better, but in order to get the most twinkle (scintillation) from the stone, it takes the candle. The twinkle makes a diamond seem to dance at the slightest movement and is very important to a diamond's character.

When diamonds come in contact with soaps and creams, their brilliancy is dimmed at once. They must be kept clean to show off at their best.

CUTTING CENTERS

The most important cutting centers are in Antwerp, Belgium, and in Israel. New York has many fine cutters, including some of the best, but they are few in comparison to the others. Holland, for years the world's leading diamond cutter, never recovered from the losses it received during the Second World War. The country has far fewer factories now, but the quality of their work is as good as it ever was.

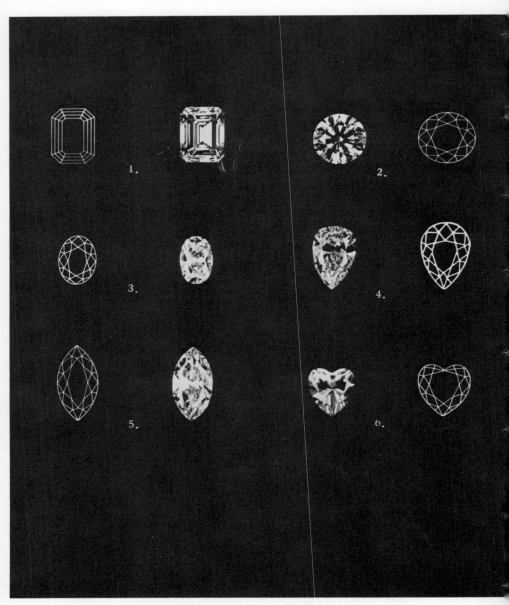

Six different styles of cut diamonds. (N.W. Ayer & Son, Inc.)

Diamonds in Industry

The greatest gift that diamonds give us is their role in industry. The industrial world would not be possible without diamonds, and they have been immensely important in the world of science. Of all the diamonds mined, 75 percent are qualified for use in industry, and only 25 percent are of gem quality, fit for jewelry and the glamour of the diamond world.

The tremendous amount of industrial diamonds is not nearly enough for the demands of the industrial world, and if it weren't for the production of synthetic diamonds in ever-increasing amounts each year, the industrial people would be in difficulty.

Efforts to synthesize diamonds go back a hundred years. Nothing was accomplished, however, until a great Swedish combine came out with a workable product. Then, General Electric Company started manufacturing synthetics and in 1955 was able to obtain world patents to cover them due to the Swedish company's failure to take proper action.

As the need for better and better diamonds grew, in 1970 General Electric came out with one of the most amazing statements ever made in the diamond world: They had succeeded in making synthetic gem-quality diamonds that were as hard as the natural ones.

There are few industries engaged in any kind of manufacture or scientific research that do not make use of industrial diamonds; and in many cases were these diamonds not available, these industrial operations would come to a complete stop. For many purposes, some synthetic material has proven superior to mined diamonds simply because their properties can be controlled and tailored for specific purposes.

Synthetic diamonds require great heat and pressure in their manufacture, approximating those of nature. Indeed, it seems to prove that diamonds were formed in Nature in the earth's mantle, where such conditions exist.

There are thousands of uses for industrial diamonds: drills of all kinds, including those used by your dentist and those used for drilling oil; diamond saws; diamond-edged knives used for sectioning biological tissues for electron microscopic examination; and diamond tools that resurface bowling balls. They are used in quarries, in much electrical equipment, and in the manufacture of automobiles, airplanes, and television sets. Some rare blue diamonds, found in South Africa, are used in unusual ways. They are used in picture telephones, a marvel used little now but sure to become very popular. They are used in radar navigation systems, computerized radar for docking the world's largest passenger and cargo vessels.

The list of uses for industrial diamonds is endless. In 1939, five million carats were used, all of them natural diamonds. In the early seventies, over fifty million carats, natural and synthetic combined, were used, and the quantity needed grows by millions of carats each year.

Diamonds are particularly needed in war times. In the Second World War, when Belgium and Holland were overrun, diamonds were among the first items to be rushed to safety.

The world of industrial diamonds may be compared to that of shipping. The luxury liners win the acclaim and admiration of the world, while the unglamorous freighters perform the essential duties of the world entirely without fanfare.

The Great Diamonds of the World

There are many diamonds that could be named in this group. Most of them are displayed with pride in the museums of the nations owning them. Here are a few of the more well-known ones.

THE HOPE DIAMOND

The most famous diamond in the United States and the largest blue diamond in the world, the Hope Diamond is the chief attraction of the Gem Room in the Smithsonian Institution in Washington, D.C.

The Hope Diamond is believed to have come from Golconda, India, and was brought to France and sold to Louis XIV in 1668. It became the principal jewel of the French Crown collection. It then weighed 112.50 carats. It was recut to improve its brilliancy, and its weight was reduced to 62.50 carats.

The Hope Diamond disappeared in the great robbery of the French Treasury in 1792 and was not recovered. Years later, in 1830, a beautiful blue diamond appeared for sale in London. It has been pretty well established that it was again recut from the one that had been stolen. The diamond was purchased by Henry Philip Hope in the same year, and it has been called the Hope Diamond ever since.

The Sultan of Turkey, Abdul Hamid II, purchased the

stone in 1908; and when he was deposed, the diamond ended up in the hands of the French jeweler Pierre Cartier. In turn, Cartier sold it to Edward McLean, whose wife, Evelyn, wore it until she died, in 1947.

The most famous gem in the United States, the Hope diamond is the largest blue diamond in existence. (N.W. Ayer & Son, Inc.)

Mrs. McLean wore the diamond happily and frequently all the time she owned it, but the stone has been associated with bad luck for many years, going back to the days of Louis XIV. Evil things happened to many who owned it; and even while it was owned by Mrs. McLean, bad luck attended members of her family.

Finally, jeweler Harry Winston bought it and later presented it to the museum that presently houses it. The great diamond was reweighed in 1975 for the first time in years, and it was found that the correct weight is 45.52 carats.

THE REGENT

The Regent is another of the famous diamonds found near Golconda, India. A slave picked up the stone in 1701. He knew it meant death if he kept it, but he slashed his leg and hid the diamond under the bandage. He fled to the seacoast and made a deal with a ship's captain for passage. Once at sea, the slave was robbed and thrown overboard.

The captain sold the diamond to an Indian merchant in 1702. The merchant offered it to Thomas Pitt, governor of Madras, India, for a half million dollars; but Pitt, who thought it had been stolen, offered $100,000 and got the diamond for that amount. Pitt was the grandfather of William Pitt, after whom Pittsburgh is named. In 1717, the diamond was sold to the Duke of Orleans, then the Regent of France, thus naming the stone. It brought more than $500,000 and eventually was placed in the crown of Louis XVI. During the French Revolution of 1792, the Regent was stolen, along with other jewels, in the great robbery of the Royal Treasury. For six nights prior to the robbery, thirty or

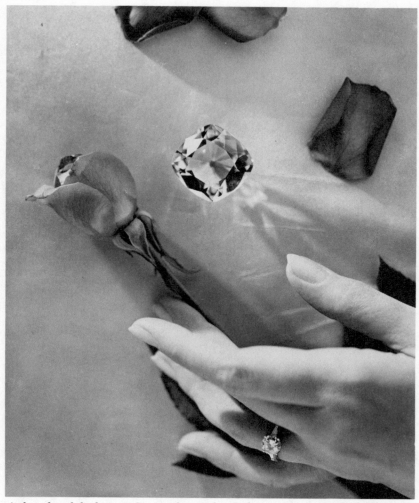

A slave found the historic Regent diamond in India in 1701. It weighed 410 carats. (N.W. Ayer & Son, Inc.)

forty bandits were reported to have entered the Treasury by using rope ladders to descend from the ceiling and hide. Many were caught and executed, and the Regent was recovered at once. At the time, it was valued at $2,500,000.

The Regent was used as a pledge to help finance Napoleon's climb to power. Five years later, the stone was redeemed, and it was mounted in Napoleon's sword for his coronation.

After Napoleon was exiled, the Regent was involved in

The greatest gem in the diamond treasury of the Soviet Union is the Orloff. (N.W. Ayer & Son, Inc.)

many political affairs. It became an established national historic piece. It is presently in the Louvre museum, in Paris.

THE ORLOFF

The greatest diamond in the Diamond Treasury of the Soviet Union is the Orloff. It came to the attention of the Western world about 1750, when it was learned that a temple in the southern part of India contained an idol with two huge diamonds for eyes. A French soldier living in the neighborhood was the first to hear about the diamonds.

No Christian was allowed in the temple, so the soldier falsely adopted the faith of the worshipers; and, after several years of faithful service, was allowed to worship in the inner shrine as a token of gratitude. After a time, he became a trusted guardian of the idol. One stormy night when no worshiper was present, he pried out one of the diamond eyes. While he was working to pry the other loose, he heard a noise and fled with only the one huge diamond.

He made his way to Madras on the Bay of Bengal and had no trouble disposing of the diamond. A British sea captain offered him $10,000 for it, and he asked no questions about how it had been obtained. In 1775, the sea captain sold the stone in London to a Persian merchant for $60,000. Finally, it was bought by Prince Gregory Orloff for $450,000.

Orloff had been one of the officers who had helped Catherine the Great seize the Russian Throne in 1762. He was one of her favorites for a long time, but with the passing years he had lost favor with her.

Orloff badly wanted to regain her favor, so he and his brothers raised the money to buy the diamond. Orloff presented the diamond to Catherine, which she accepted happily. She loved diamonds and had a very large collection of them. But she never reinstated Orloff to his former high position. It was a gamble that lost.

The diamond weighs 189.62 carats, is shaped like "half of a hard-boiled egg," and is in the royal scepter in the Kremlin of the U.S.S.R., in Moscow.

THE KOHINOOR

Probably the most notorious and famous diamond in the world is the Kohinoor. In 1304, it was owned by the Rajah of Malwa in India. Sultan Baber, first of the Mogul emperors, acquired it in 1526 after his son defeated the Rajah of Gwalior, who owned it at the time. Each reigning Mogul inherited the diamond, including Shah Jehan, who built the Taj Mahal. The diamond remained in India until 1739, when Delhi was sacked by Nadir Shah. Unable to locate the gem after months of searching, he finally learned the secret from one of the girls of the harem of Mohammed Shah. The diamond was hidden in the turban of the Shah, and he never removed it, no matter where he went. Nadir Shah could easily have killed him at any time, and it isn't clear why he didn't do so. Instead, Nadir invited Mohammed to a very elaborate affair at which he reinstated the Mogul Sultan and vowed eternal friendship. At this point, Nadir Shah asked the Mogul to exchange turbans as a mark of eternal friendship. The turbans were exchanged, as there was no graceful way to refuse. Nadir Shah immediately went to his tent, undid the turban feverishly, and there it was! He exclaimed, "Kohinoor!" meaning "mountain of light" in Persian, and so it was named.

Nadir Shah was assassinated, and the stone went to his

Queen Mary's Crown is set with the famous Kohinoor and Cullinans' III and IV, products of the Cullinan rough. (British Information Service.)

son, who greatly loved the stone and stared at it by the hour. When he was to be deposed, he hid the diamond. Although horribly tortured, he did not reveal his secret.

The stone passed from ruler to ruler, sometimes by inheritance, sometimes by force. Finally, Ranjit Singh got it by promising sanctuary to the one who owned it at the time. He wore it in a bracelet for years, then had it reset. After Ranjit died, it remained in the treasury of the Punjab of Lahore.

After a mutinous affair led to the annexation of the

Punjab to the British Empire, the diamond was presented to Queen Victoria. She had it recut. The cutting job was poor, and the diamond was reduced in weight. It is now on display in a crown in the Tower of London, in England.

DARYA-I-NUR

The most famous diamond in the land of Iran, formerly Persia, is the Darya-I-Nur. Iran has one of the greatest collections of diamonds and precious gems in the world. This diamond, which weighs about 175 carats or more, is the largest pink diamond there is, and it is one of the most valuable. Originally, it came from the great Golconda mines of India. Nadir Shah brought it to Persia when he returned after his plunder of the palaces in Delhi in 1739. Two years after his return with wagon loads of booty, Nadir was assassinated.

The best-known gem in Iran, Darya-i-Nur, the "sea of light," part of the booty from the sack of Delhi in 1739. (Royal Ontario Museum.)

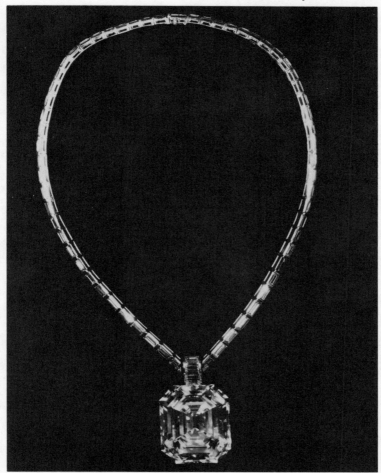

The Jonker diamond, found in the mud in South Africa by Jacobus Jonker in 1934. He sold the stone for $315,000.

JONKER

Jacobus Jonker, a veteran but luckless digger for most of his sixty-two years, was walking on his farm near Pretoria, South Africa, after a heavy rainstorm, hoping against hope that this might be the day when he would find that big diamond he had always dreamed about. And, suddenly, there it was! He wasn't sure it was real; he had never seen anything like it. He and his family got no sleep that night for their excitement. The diamond turned out to be the seventh largest ever found; and a few days later he sold it for $315,000.

The cutting of this stone proved to be very complex. Cutters the world over disagreed about how it should be done. Fortunately, it was done correctly. In 1972, the largest diamond cut from this stone was sold for $3,500,000—one of the highest prices ever paid for a single cut diamond.

IDOL'S EYE

A beautiful diamond found in the famous Golconda fields in India at the beginning of the seventeenth century, this stone was once the eye of a sacred idol. It became the property of Persian prince Rahib early in its history. The prince owed money to the East India Company, who seized the diamond for nonpayment in 1607. It disappeared from public view for exactly three hundred years. In 1907, it was discovered to be in the possession of Sultan Abdul Hamid II. He was having troubles at home at that time, so he conspired with his Grand Vizier to smuggle the diamond, along with others, out of the country.

The messenger was supposedly robbed on the train in a tale worthy of the best TV tradition of today. But the facts have not been proved. We do know, however, that the diamond finally showed up in Paris and was sold to a Spanish nobleman. It is in the United States at the present time, one of the few great diamonds in our country.

THE SANCY

The Sancy is a beautiful diamond of 55 carats and one of

the first with facets of symmetry. The French ambassador to Turkey, the Seigneur de Sancy, purchased it in Constantinople in about 1570. He lent it to his king, Henry III, who wore it in a cap to hide his baldness. His successor, Henry IV, who

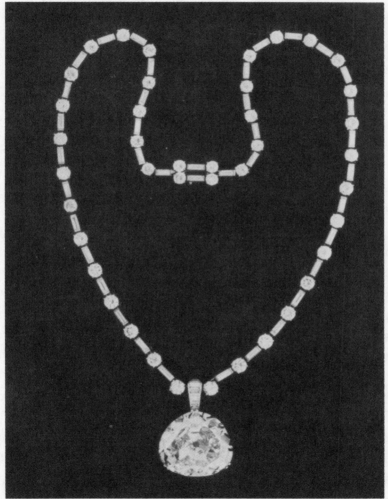

The Idol's Eye, a beautiful white diamond, was found in the famous Golconda fields in India. (N.W. Ayer & Son, Inc.)

The Sancy diamond once adorned a cap that Henry III wore to conceal his baldness.

needed money to raise an army, used the diamond to cover the loan. On the way to the bank, the messenger was attacked by robbers. He swallowed the diamond to save it from the bandits, but he was killed. The diamond was recovered from his body.

Queen Elizabeth I of England bought it, and it remained in England for fifty years. When James II became king, he lost everything, including his kingdom, in a great battle. But he held onto the diamond and fled to France. Louis XIV paid a large sum for the stone, and it proved to be a godsend for the fallen James. The Sancy became part of the French Crown Jewels, and although it was stolen in the great robbery of the French Treasury, it was ultimately recovered. After many more changes of country, it was sold to William Waldorf Astor, and it is believed to be in his family at present.

SHAH

A bar-shaped diamond originally found in India, this stone had engraved on it three markings giving the names of owners and dates. One owner was Shah Jahan, who built the Taj Mahal. It is not known for sure how the diamond got to Persia from India, but is is entirely possible that Nadir Shah took it when he robbed and pillaged India in 1739.

The Shah diamond was offered by the Persian government as a peace gesture to Czar Nicholas I following the assassination of the Russian ambassador to Teheran in 1829. (De Beers Consolidated Mines Ltd.)

Petrus Ramaboa proudly holds the Lesotho diamond, a 601.25-carat stone that his wife found on their 30-foot-square claim.

While this great diamond was in the hands of Persian rulers, an inscription was made on the stone, giving the name of the ruler "Kadjar Fath Ali Shah," who was Shah of Persia in 1824.

In 1829, the Russian ambassador to Teheran was assassinated by Persians. The diamond was given to Czar Nicholas I of Russia by the Persian government to partially make amends, thereby saving them from what could have been a war between nations. The Shah became one of the treasured jewels of the Russians, and it is in the Kremlin, in Moscow at this time. The weight is given at 88.70 carats.

LESOTHO

Formerly called Basutoland, the nation of Lesotho made headlines in 1967, when a very large diamond was found there. It weighed, in its original state, 601.25 carats, making it one of the eleven largest ever found. The owners of a very small claim, thirty feet square, had worked hard on the property for five years, averaging a dollar a day by finding a few tiny diamonds.

One fine day, Ernestine Ramaboa, the wife of the owner, found the diamond, "large as an egg." The husband put the stone in his pocket and they walked and hitchhiked to the capital, Maseru. They sold their diamond for over $300,000.